Hidden in PLAIN SIGHT

Images,
Words,
and
Reflections

ANOUSHKA SHARMA

Archway Publishing books may be ordered through booksellers or by contacting:

Archway Publishing
1663 Liberty Drive
Bloomington, IN 47403
www.archwaypublishing.com
1 (888) 242-5904

Because of the dynamic nature of the Internet, any web addresses or links contained in this book may have changed since publication and may no longer be valid. The views expressed in this work are solely those of the author and do not necessarily reflect the views of the publisher, and the publisher hereby disclaims any responsibility for them.

This book is a work of non-fiction. Unless otherwise noted, the author and the publisher make no explicit guarantees as to the accuracy of the information contained in this book and in some cases, names of people and places have been altered to protect their privacy.

Any people depicted in stock imagery provided by Getty Images are models, and such images are being used for illustrative purposes only.
Certain stock imagery © Getty Images.

ISBN: 978-1-4808-7317-9 (sc)
ISBN: 978-1-4808-7318-6 (e)

Print information available on the last page.

Archway Publishing rev. date: 4/12/2019

Table of Contents

Preface

Is it not the case that there is always some measurable difference between what we think we see and what is actually there? Even our most contrary emotions are often two sides of the same coin. Anoushka Sharma's poems negotiate the trapeze that hangs by light and dark, presence and absence, pain and forgiveness; swinging, as it were, one way now, and another way then. Her poem "Speechless" acknowledges this paradox: "Words/They're everything I love/And hate/At the same time."

Anoushka's poems breathe slowly and think inwardly. Each is an observation deck from which the reader looks upon the unexpected similarities within the differences between one experience and another. "I don't know what to say/I just want to know if I'm brave," one poem requests. "I want to know the things that grow to be/Amazing in the world." These yearnings are surface water atop the deep well of concerns that are central to our human condition: Are the obstacles we perceive internal or external? Do we have the power to recreate ourselves? Even if others give us the space to move on, will we allow ourselves to?

It has been my good fortune to be Anoushka's English teacher for two years at Chapin School in Princeton, New Jersey. Her identity as a reader and writer is strong, and her classmates look forward to the time that they share with her. No matter what she grows up to be, her consideration for her audience will add value anywhere she goes.

In the collection of poems presented here, her growth over the past five years is reflected. Anoushka has been writing since she was eight years old. Now fourteen, her thoughts and feelings are expressed with greater clarity. People who appreciate the power of words, both young and old, will find meaning and purpose in these poems. As she matures into an adult, her words will continue to find resonance in people's hearts and minds as her love of poetry evolves into a constant source of wonder and meaning.

Shawn J. Berger – Princeton, New Jersey
December 2018

Sunshine (2012)

I walked to the edge of the side walk and this is what I see
The sun is shining right on me
Everything around me is bright, it's alright
Don't be in fright
When the sun is shining on me everything will be alright
Everything will be alright

Moonlight (2012)

Yesterday was once tomorrow
Tomorrow will be yesterday
It may come with lots of sorrow
Or something I just can't say

Oh what a beautiful sight, here tonight
It just makes me wanna say

It's ok, it's alright,
Dancing in the moonlight
It's ok, it's alright now

Don't stop, keep going,
Through anything you're doing
It's ok, it's alright now

Sweet Love Birds (2014)

Oh sweet love birds, I know you're here

So come and take me, on the path of joyous tears

Oh sweet love birds, I know you're here

So come out, and let us all cheer

How do you disguise

Beauty in feathers of white

And who knew a word called love,

Could come from a dove

Oh sweet love birds, a creature I adore

Oh sweet love birds, be ,mine and I'll be yours!

Friendship (2014)

Some days are tough
and there's no one to pass the love
To my side of the table

But when I'm down
I turn around
and you're there

So when your day's not going well
I'll be there for you too

Take my hand
our journey has just begun
We can rule the world together
as one
Every time, we sit side by side
I fall into your friendship another time
So gather around the fire,
And snap along to the song,
because no one can tear us apart

Happy (2015)

When I'm happy I like to sing
When I'm happy I don't care what people think
When I am happy I feel so loved
I watch the clouds fade from the sky above
When I am happy I never imagine feeling blue
But most of all I always think of you

A Land of Hope (2015)

Some days can be tough
You just want to cry
You're drenched in a puddle of sadness
But you don't know why
For some reason, the window of hope closed
How to open it? No one really knows
But the puddle only grows
Into a river then and ocean
You find yourself floating
Atop a tide of tears
But suddenly the sadness becomes shallow
You reach land
A land of laughter
A land of love
A land of hope.

Me, Myself and I (2015)

I know you think I'm crazy
and maybe it's true

I know you think I'm weird
but so are you

You think I don't know
but I hear all the gossip

You should know that I'm not going to change who I am

I don't care what you say
I'm not listening anyway

Why don't you spare all the talk
Time is ticking on the clock

I am who I am
That's not going to change

Someday I will fly
By being me, myself and I

A Bird Without Wings (2016)

I have not yet reached the mountain top
But I am climbing

I have not completed every chapter
But I am writing

I might be losing every game,
But I'm still smiling

I have not taken my last footsteps
A long journey has yet to find me

I may be the last in line,
That means I push others along

I may not be able to rhyme,
But I can surely sing a song

I finish last in every race,
But I never stopped trying

But I'm a bird without wings
Who'll always wish she were flying

The Sun (2016)

I lay awake with the sounds of working men,
With the howl of restless dogs
With the sudden chirp of the morning birds,
The birds that fly to welcome the sun
The sun which glows through the hotel curtain
I listen to my brother toss and turn in his deep sleep
The sun that glows wakes my brother
The sun which summons bicycle bells and car horns
The sun that glows will glow for a while

You Need Wings To Fly (2016)

Everybody wants to make their mark
Everybody wants to touch the sky
Everybody wants to find that spark
But we all need wings to fly

All the little girls who want to change the world
All the little boys who always try
Everybody wants to find that spark
But we all need wings to fly

When wounds may seem too deep too mend,
Don't ever think you've reached your end

Everybody wants to make their mark
Everybody wants to touch the sky
Everybody wants to find that spark
We all need wings to fly

So even when life gets tough
It's okay to cry
Everybody has to find their spark
We all need wings to fly

Destiny (2016)

Look at me
I am free to do anything I want
I'm ready for everything that comes my way

Remember me
I'm the girl you used to know
The girl whom you thought couldn't do a single thing

I'll show the world
That I'm not just a girl
From a small town

I'll show the world
That I'm not a girl
Whose dreams will end up lost and never found

So I'll climb the highest mountain around
I'll swim the deepest sea there is
My feet can't ever touch the ground
I'll make my dreams come true
That's what my destiny is

I'll Do It My Own Way (2016)

I know you think I'm not the type of girl who's
Gonna make a change in the world

But I can definitely tell you
that you've
Got me wrong
I've got dreams, hopes and a plan for the future
I'm gonna make things work

And not a single person
Can stop me today
 I will change the world
And I'll do it my own way.

For A Day (2016)

Always criticized
always stepped on like a rug

Always pushed aside
all alone with no one to hug

But she always tries, you'll never see her frown
says she never cries, but she does when the sun goes down

She's not perfect
she might not be worth it
She's not special, but still

She's kind anyway
and she tries everyday

She always does anything anyone wants her to do

She doesn't fuss over things
she doesn't need diamond rings

She just wants happiness
for a day

A Second Chance (2016)

If I were given a second chance,
To do my life over again,
I'd certainly take it.
I'd live each moment to the fullest
I'd take advantage of rare experiences,
And spend more time with the ones who care for me
I'd break through the chains of "what if…"
And run free letting my hair flow in the breeze
I'd seize each moment, and maybe fall down too,
But I'd pick myself up and continue
So if I were given a second chance to do my life over again,
I'd cherish each breath and not waste it,
Wishing each day never ends

Hush (2016)

A room filled with noises and voices chattering away,
But I stay waiting with my eyes closed
I cover my ears and suddenly "Hush"
The sweet sound of nothing,
Thickening the air
Just me and the pumping of my heart
No birds chirping
No feet stomping
Only the simplicity of my thoughts
A moment of me, myself, and I that I'll always cherish
As if this moment is just a dream,
For it all disappears as I uncover my ears and
Expose myself to a world of boisterous clatter.

Front Door (2016)

I don't know what to say
I just want to know if I'm brave
I want to know the things that grow to be
Amazing in the world

I don't know anymore
I want to know what's beyond my front door
I want to know if there's still hope

I need to know
I need to know

I want to know what's beyond my front door
I want to see beyond the world I know

I see it now
I see it now

Now I know I'm brave
I can be who I want in the world

Nothing else matters anymore
There's a whole new world beyond my front door

I Made Her Smile (2016)

There was a girl who lived a few houses down the road
Whenever I'd see her she was always on her own
When she'd walk down the street
I'd wonder where she'd go
But at that time I didn't know how much
It would mean if I said hello

I saw her at school the next week
She was alone at lunch with nothing to eat
So I grabbed my things and left my friends
I made my way to her end
of the room
She looked shy,
But I said hi
And I was surprised
She told me her name

She told me she lost her parents a while back
She told me she really missed her mom and dad
She lived with her grandma
She had no friends at all
She was new in town
And she was glad I sat down

I didn't know her story
I didn't know her part
I didn't know how much it hurts
I didn't know her heart
And I thought to myself it's so clear now
I hope she knows it's all worth while
I hope she knows I'm by her side
I hope she's glad I made her smile

A Note From Your Little Girl (2017)

Just as a flower blooms
You held out your arms for me
Just as a fire burns
You set off a spark in me
Just as the rain cools you
You always stay calm with me
And even though I let you down
I hope you can see
I'm grateful for all that you've done for me

Your Name (2017)

I wrote your name on my heart
But how do I erase the scars
That you gave me when you
Said your last goodbye

I don't want fame, don't wanna be a star
As long as you stay right where you are
But where you are is far away
It used to feel good to hear you say my name
But now I only feel the pain

You left the room without a word
A voice I never heard
You said you'd be here forever
But it's just me and the cold weather

I wish it never happened
I wish you never walked in
It felt like the world was burning down
But I know not to walk into the flames now

I don't want your name on my heart
So you can stay right where you are
You think I am weak, but I am strong
Now you can see, I'm moving on

Mama (2017)

Your heels stand high, but the feet inside are weary
A thousand secrets, your plastered smile may carry
Your tired eyes, disguised, behind some eye shadow
Not everyone sees this, but I certainly know

I always think you're ready for whatever comes your way
You always seem to know just what to say
You tackle everything, big or small
But you're only human, after all

Mama,
I see you crying
You say you are fine
I know you're lying

You never tell me what's true
And I just don't know what to do
Sometimes I hurt,
Don't see my worth
But you seem worse

I just want to help you through
Whatever you are going through

Maybe I can help you
Maybe you can help me
I can hold your hand as we travel along on this journey
I don't want you to feel lonely
I'm not saying I should be your only
I just want you to hold me tight, Mama
And say you love me.

Through The Clouds and To The Sun (2017)

I'm sitting in a noisy room
With crums on my plate
It's about. …half past noon
The table around me,
Still filled with food
The one to my left,
Slurping the last bubbles of a grape juice box
The one to my right
Failing to finish a tuna slider
But my mind is in the clouds
Barely holding myself in my seat,
Waiting for recess to come
My mind is in the clouds
Longing to be in the sky
Waiting to take flight
Waiting to swing, to and fro and to and fro……
To feel the wind….
Against my cheeks
To feel my long dark locks
Brush the dirt, as I lean back towards the ground
When we get outside
I close my eyes
And when they open again
I find that the wind has pushed me
One step closer,
To the sun

Mother (2017)

Your kiss is a soft cloud
Caressing my forehead
Your hug, like the scorching sun,
Melting my heart
Your voice, as sharp as an eagle's claw
But as sweet as a nightingale's song

Your tears, the tranquil rains
Descending in the trees
Only bringing your smile,
The rainbow after the storm

Your laugh echoes through the rubble
And ruin of old broken church bells
Your mind,
The only thing strong enough
To push open the gates of self-doubt

And no matter the weather
Your eyes glisten
And shine like the only candle
Left burning through the darkest night

Artist
Anoushka Sharma '19

Artist
Anoushka Sharma
Grade 5

Speechless (2018)

Words
They're everything I love
And hate
At the same time
Sometimes
They pour out of me
Other times
They stop
Like a drought
No more water
No more words

Words build me up
And break me down
Like they say
Sticks and stones
May break my bones
But words…

Wait

No

Words do hurt me
They bring
Tears
Smiles
Sadness
Joy
Until the drought is back

No more words
No more me

Always Been You (2018)

It's always been you
You
The thing inside me
Holding me back
You
The voice in my head
Saying no
You
A treat
So sweet outside
Yet so sour within
It's you
Always
The cancer
In me
Killing me
Slowly
Softly
With every breath
And the worst part is
I let you

Butterflies (2018)

I remember the feeling
sweaty palms
biting my nails
pacing,
back
and forth
a distant voice
says my name
and suddenly I'm moving,
it's all in a blur
my feet are moving
but at the same time
they aren't
and I find myself
standing center stage
feeling like the smallest thing on earth
big bright lights
all on me
and big bright eyes
all on me
I look to the back of the room
and see a camera flashing
my parents,
of course
but it doesn't make me feel any better
the slightest touch of air on my skin
sends a frightening chill down my spine
and I can feel the little hairs on my arms,
rising
I clear my throat
take a breath
exhale
I place my hands on the microphone
and start to sing
everything fades away

My Escape (2018)

It's the music
That I turn to
Not the people
Not the places
No
It's the music
It brings me silence
In its volume
It drowns everything out
The clicking of pens
The clatter of keyboards
The laughter of children
The shrieks of pain
The scratches of a chalkboard
The soft,
Faint sound
of breath

I turn to the music
When the pain
In my heart
Is too loud
For my ears

So when the places disappear
And the people run away
It's the music
That lifts me up
And carries me
To a place where my heart
Hums a tranquil tune

Perfectly Flawed (2018)

Next time you draw
A picture of me
Please don't make it perfect
Because when you accept the flaws in me
You'll realize how much I'm worth it

Hey, Girls (2018)

I can't take it anymore
Everywhere I go
I see girls...
Taking selfies
Wearing makeup
Trying to impress
Someone or another
I feel sick to my stomach
When I see
That this is all we are
After years of fighting
For what we deserve
Shouldn't we girls
Let our voices be heard?
But no
Stay quiet
Don't say a word
Just bring it all on
Eyeshadow
Lipstick
Blush
Everything
Put on a fake smile
Look pretty
Who cares if we aren't smart
Or witty
We're pretty
Remember?
And that seems to be
All that matters
So keep on your makeup
Post that last selfie
If this is all
You want to be

The Way We Are (2018)

I work, you win
You're gold, I'm tin
I cry, you smile
I run, the extra mile
I walk, you're flying
You love me?
Stop lying.

When Little Girls Grow Up (2018)

'She was a little girl once'
Said the mother
Her hair gray
Her eyes tired

'But of course she was
We all were once
I remember her
Innocent
And free
My little princess
That, was she'

She closed her eyes
Fell back in her chair
And sighed

'Slowly but sweetly
She grew
As all little girls do
I longed so deeply
To keep her in my arms
But she broke free
But I know I couldn't have stopped her?'
She blinked
I couldn't have stopped a thing
I watched the seed of a girl blossom
Into a flower
An independent woman'

'And sure
I missed her
When she went away to live her life
When she didn't return
For winter holidays
Or long weekends
Birthdays
Or summers
Or ever'

'And sure
I cried
When I looked
At her pictures
I still do'

A tear trickled down
Her wrinkled cheek

'I had to accept
That my
Little princess
Was finding her own kingdom
Making the world
Her home'

She wiped her eyes
Her face, wet and soppy
'Maybe someday
She'll have a little girl
Of her own'
She sighed
'And like all princesses do
She'll grow
Into a queen'

Wanderer (2018)

a sea
a quiet sea
stretching its long arms
far and wide
flowing deep
deep blue

and far too deep...

a small boat
wandering
carrying a wanderer
adrift
with drifting thoughts
feelings unfelt
emotions unseen
a purpose never found

twisted images come alive
the darkest shadows destroy all light
a nightmare never ending
make it stop
I'm holding my breath
but can't let go

exhale
and it's gone
like dust blown away
all under my control

and
all that's left
is a wanderer
wandering

Dear Mom and Dad (2018)

I really hope you know, how much I care
Even though some days, that might not seem true
And even on those days, when you want to pull out your hair
Just remember, that I'll always love you

Or even the days, when you feel life is unfair
Or when you're sad and you don't know why
Just remember, I'll always be there
To wipe every tear when you cry

And yes there are days when I misbehave
And I drive you crazy too
But just remember, that in every which way
I'll always love you

Far Away Together (2018)

I'm sitting here
Outside
I see everything
And nothing
All at once
The birds
They chirp
But what do they say
The leaves
They rustle
But why
Why
Tell me
Why you aren't here
To enjoy this moment
With me
I'm sitting here
Watching the flowers bloom
With all the time in the world
I hear you

Everywhere
In the birds
In the leaves
I see you
The flowers
Resemble
Everything you are
But why
All this time
Just fell into my lap
This time
To just sit
Here
Alone
Everything is here
I have everything
Don't I?
But it feels
Like nothing
Without you

Endorsements

Steph Hon

"Anoushka Sharma is very mature for her age, and sees things many people don't. I want to keep reading her writing! It's so powerful that she is sharing what is in her heart and mind, and she is inspiring me to think and be more grounded. She is creating so much power through her words and pictures. We need people of her generation to continue to examine, question, and talk about what they see happening around them. She is a strong voice inspiring each of us to connect back to our sense of wonder and confidence to create change."

Tanya Vail

"Perspective can change everything. Anoushka's unique artistic perspective provides a thought provoking balm for the soul through a compelling blend of words and images. Her deeply evocative works are a refreshing new look at subjects that are relatable to everyone. Anoushka's powerful creative voice provides inspiration for examining ourselves and the rich experience of discovering the wider world."

Liz Leach

"When I was asked to read Anoushka Sharma's poetry book, I had no idea what I would discover therein. What an unexpected delight I found: a hidden treasure revealed before my eyes! Anoushka's anthology of poems, Hidden in Plain Sight, represents about five years of profound reflections written between the ages 8-13, in which one can follow the trajectory of her personal development. This work offers both depth of consciousness and the vibrancy of the sensations and feelings of aliveness as a girl progresses through awakening to both herself and her full spectrum of experiences in life, experiences both within and without. Through the power of word, Anoushka finds her voice and discovers how to take flight in a world she learns can be both exhilarating and challenging, painful and inspiring. It speaks to the ways in which writing and poetry can unlock potential, empower and unleash awareness in today's youth—setting a tremendous example. This little gem is a great read for adults and children alike."

Printed in the United States
By Bookmasters